P9-CEQ-470

Penny
AND HER MARBLE

KEVIN HENKES

GREENWILLOW BOOKS
An Imprint of HarperCollins*Publishers*

Watercolor paints and a black pen were used to prepare the full-color art.

The text type is 17-point Century Schoolbook.

I Can Read Book® is a trademark of HarperCollins Publishers Inc.

Penny and Her Marble

Copyright © 2013 by Kevin Henkes

All rights reserved. Manufactured in China. For information address HarperCollins Children's Books,

a division of HarperCollins Publishers, 10 East 53rd Street, New York, NY 10022.

www.harpercollinschildrens.com

Library of Congress Cataloging-in-Publication Data

Henkes, Kevin.

Penny and her marble / by Kevin Henkes.

p. cm.

"Greenwillow Books."

Summary: Penny feels guilty after taking a beautiful blue marble that she sees in

Mrs. Goodwin's grass, but gets a pleasant surprise when she goes to return it the next day.

ISBN 978-0-06-208203-9 (trade ed.)

ISBN 978-0-06-208204-6 (lib. ed.)—ISBN 978-0-06-208205-3 (pbk.)

[1. Lost and found possessions—Fiction. 2. Marbles—Fiction. 3. Mice—Fiction.] I. Title.

PZ7.H389Pei 2012   [E]—dc23   2012000708

13 14 15 16 17 SCP 10 9 8 7 6 5 4 3 2 1

First Edition

GREENWILLOW BOOKS

To Penny and Ford

Chapter 1

Penny was pushing her doll, Rose,

in her stroller.

They went back and forth

on the front sidewalk.

"Only go as far

as Mrs. Goodwin's house,"

called Mama.

Penny pretended they were
in a big city.
"Look at the tall buildings, Rose,"
said Penny.

When they got

to Mrs. Goodwin's house,

they turned around.

Then Penny pretended

they were in a forest.

"I hope we don't get lost

in the trees, Rose," she said.

They went back and forth
again and again.

Now Penny pretended
they were flying in a plane.
"Everything looks so tiny
from up here," said Penny.

Just then Penny saw something

on Mrs. Goodwin's lawn.

It glinted in the sun.

It was a marble.

A big, shiny blue marble.

It can't be Mrs. Goodwin's,

thought Penny.

She is too old to play

with a marble.

Penny bent down

to get a better look.

The marble seemed to say,

"Take me home."

Penny looked around.

No one was watching.

Penny picked up the marble.

She put the marble

in her pocket.

Then Penny raced home
with Rose.

Chapter 2

Penny took the marble
to her room.

She shut the door.

Penny rolled the marble
between her fingers.

The marble was smooth.

Penny rolled the marble
across the floor.

The marble was fast.

Penny showed the marble to Rose.

"Isn't it pretty, Rose?"

said Penny.

The marble was so blue

it looked like a piece

of the sky.

Penny went to the window

and held up the marble.

She was right.

The marble *was*

like a piece of the sky.

Penny saw Mrs. Goodwin
out the window.
Mrs. Goodwin was in
her yard.
Mrs. Goodwin was exactly
where Penny had found
the marble.

Penny hid

behind the curtain.

Was Mrs. Goodwin

looking for the marble?

Penny left the window.

She hid the marble

in her dresser.

Penny stayed by Mama

and the babies all afternoon.

She could not stop thinking

about the marble.

Chapter 3

"Do you want to bake cookies?" asked Mama.

Penny shrugged.

"We could make your favorites," said Mama. "Sugar cookies."

"I'll watch you," said Penny.

"Are you feeling okay?"
asked Mama.
"My stomach hurts a little,"
said Penny.
Mama felt Penny's forehead.
"No fever," said Mama.

Penny watched Mama

bake cookies.

Penny helped a little.

At dinner,

Penny did not eat much.

The oranges in the bowl

looked like big orange marbles.

The peas on her plate

looked like little green marbles.

Penny pushed the peas

around her plate.

"I am not hungry,"

she said.

Penny did not want

a sugar cookie for dessert.

At bedtime, Mama said,

"You still do not have a fever."

Papa said, "You will feel better

in the morning."

"It's probably just a bug,"

said Penny.

"Are you worried about something?"
asked Mama.

"No," said Penny.

"Are you sure?" asked Papa.

Penny nodded.

After Mama and Papa

left her room,

Penny looked at the marble.

It was still so blue

and so smooth

and so shiny.

Penny put the marble

back in her dresser.

Penny could not sleep.

She kept thinking

about the marble.

When Penny did fall asleep,

she dreamed.

She dreamed that Mrs. Goodwin

was knocking on the door,

yelling, "Where is my marble?"

Then Penny dreamed

that the marble grew so big

it broke her dresser to bits.

Finally Penny stopped dreaming.

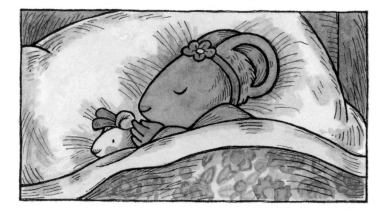

She slept deeply until morning.

Chapter 4

When Penny woke up,
she had forgotten
about the marble.
All of a sudden,
she remembered.

Penny got dressed quickly.

She got the marble

and put it in her pocket.

Penny looked for Mama.

"Mama?" said Penny. "May I take Rose
for a walk before breakfast?"
"Are you feeling better today?"
asked Mama.
Penny nodded.
"Okay," said Mama. "Just to
Mrs. Goodwin's and back."

Penny pushed Rose
to Mrs. Goodwin's yard.

Penny could feel the marble
in her pocket.
It felt as heavy
as a rock.

Penny bent down.

She put the marble

back where she had found it.

"Let's go home, Rose,"

said Penny. "Hurry."

"Wait!" called Mrs. Goodwin.

Penny's heart pounded.

"Oh, Penny, don't you want

that pretty blue marble?"

Penny looked up
at Mrs. Goodwin.
Penny's cheeks were hot.
She could not speak.

Mrs. Goodwin said, "I found
the marble yesterday.
It was in the back
of my kitchen drawer.
I thought someone
would love it.
That is why I put it
on the grass
by the sidewalk."

"I hoped someone would
walk by and see it," she said.

"I did see it," said Penny.
"But I thought
it was yours,
so I put it back."

Mrs. Goodwin picked up
the marble.
She put the marble
in Penny's hand.
"And now it is *yours*,"
said Mrs. Goodwin.
"Thank you!" said Penny.
"Thank you very much!"

Penny rolled the marble

between her fingers.

It seemed even more shiny

and smooth

and blue than before.

"Have a good day,"

said Mrs. Goodwin.

"I will," said Penny. "I will."

Penny pushed Rose home.

Penny pretended they were

in a boat on the sea.

"The sea is the same color

as my marble," said Penny.

Penny pushed faster.

"This boat ride is making me
hungry, Rose," said Penny.
"Let's go inside and have
the biggest and best
breakfast ever."

And they did.